Voice of Freedom

Voice of Freedom

A Story about Frederick Douglass

by Maryann N. Weidt
illustrated by Jeni Reeves

A Creative Minds Biography

Carolrhoda Books, Inc./Minneapolis

To my writers group—Linda Glaser, Katharine Johnson, Sue Larson, Margi Preus, and Ann Treacy. Thanks for listening. — M. W.

The author thanks: Joy Kinard at the Frederick Douglass National Historic Site for taking the time to answer all my questions. Special thanks to Jill Braithwaite and Kari Cornell, two very fine editors.

The illustrator thanks: Joseph McGill and the African American Heritage Museum, Cedar Rapids, IA; Ruth Rosenberg-Naparsteck, City Historian, Rochester Public Library, Rochester, NY; Kenneth A. McClane, Jr., W.E.B. Dubois Professor of Literature, Cornell University, Ithaca, NY; Laurence Burgess of Cedar Hill, Frederick Douglass National Historic Site; Frank Faragasso, National Park Service; Dr. Paul F. Johnston, Curator of Maritime History, Smithsonian Museum of American History, Washington, D.C.

Text copyright © 2001 by Maryann N. Weidt
Illustrations copyright © 2001 by Jeni Reeves

This book is available in two editions:
Library binding by Carolrhoda Books, Inc.,
    a division of Lerner Publishing Group
Softcover by First Avenue Editions,
    an imprint of Lerner Publishing Group
241 First Avenue North
Minneapolis, Minnesota 55401 U.S.A.

Website address: www.lernerbooks.com

Library of Congress Cataloging-in-Publication Data

Weidt, Maryann N.
    Voice of freedom: a story about Frederick Douglass / by Maryann N. Weidt; illustrations by Jeni Reeves.
        p.   cm. — (A creative minds biography)
    Includes bibliographical references and index.
    ISBN 1-57505-459-0 (lib. bdg. : alk. paper)
    ISBN 1-57505-553-8 (pbk.: alk. paper)
    1. Douglass, Frederick 1817?–1895—Juvenile literature. 2. Abolitionists—United States—Biography—Juvenile literature. 3. Afro-American abolitionists—Biography—Juvenile literature. 4. Antislavery movements—United States—Juvenile literature. [1. Douglass, Frederick, 1817? –1895. 2. Abolitionists. 3. Afro-Americans—Biography.] I. Reeves, Jeni, ill. II. Title. III. Series.
E449.D75 W43 2001
973.8'092—dc21   00-009731

Manufactured in the United States of America
1 2 3 4 5 6 – MA – 06 05 04 03 02 01

Table of Contents

Cold and Hungry   7

Determined to Read   14

A Step Back   20

A Powerful Speaker   35

Freedom for All   39

To Live Respectably   50

Bibliography   60

Index   62

1

Cold and Hungry

Four-year-old Frederick Bailey splashed in the cool water of the Tuckahoe Creek. A turtle snapped nearby. Frederick poked at it with a stick, trying to get the turtle to play with him. When Frederick tired of playing in the creek, he ambled over to the chicken coop. Cluck, cluck, said the chickens. Cluck, cluck, echoed Frederick. Next he visited the pigs and the goats. He imitated their sounds, too.

At the end of the day, Frederick made his way back home—his grandparents' cabin on the creek's banks. Each night he climbed up the ladder to the loft he shared with his cousins. They'd snuggle together and whisper until they drifted off to sleep.

Sometimes if Frederick had trouble falling asleep, he'd think about his home. Frederick loved the Tuckahoe Creek. And he loved the people who lived on its banks. His grandmother, Betsey Bailey, had taken care of him since he was a baby. Frederick's mother, Harriet Bailey, had given birth to him in

Grandmother's cabin. Frederick knew where he had been born, but he did not know when. No one kept track of slaves' birthdates.

Frederick did not know who his father was. Although he had heard that his father was a white man, he never learned who he was. That rumor made no difference in Frederick's status, however. Harriet Bailey was a slave, so Frederick was a slave, too.

Aaron Anthony owned most of Frederick's family. Anthony worked for Colonel Edward Lloyd, a former governor of Maryland. This meant that Anthony's slaves had to obey the orders of Edward Lloyd, too. Frederick lived on Edward Lloyd's plantation in Talbot County, Maryland. The Lloyd farms produced mostly wheat, corn, oats, wool, and tobacco. And slaves did most of the work.

Frederick's mother, Harriet, worked some twelve miles away, so Frederick rarely saw her. It was common for masters to separate slave mothers from their children. Edward Lloyd allowed Frederick's grandmother, Betsey, to care for her grandchildren. Betsey's daughters were then free to work in the fields every day.

But Frederick was in good hands. His grandmother was well respected, especially for her farming expertise. She taught neighbors how to grow sweet potatoes. Folks paid Betsey with vegetables.

Grandmother Bailey knew about fishing, too. She fished for shad and herring and wove her own nets to catch them. Sometimes she sold the nets to people in nearby towns. Frederick's grandfather, Isaac, was a freeman. He cut wood for a living. The Baileys were poor, but they had enough to eat. Frederick was happy living with his grandparents.

Then one day in August, when Frederick was about six, everything changed. His grandmother told him they were going for a long walk. Frederick asked his grandmother where they were going. She didn't answer. They walked for miles down a dusty road, past fields of yellow wheat. Frederick clung to his grandmother's hand. After a while, Frederick became very thirsty. But there was no water to drink.

He grew so tired he could not walk. His grandmother picked him up and carried him. They had walked about twelve miles when Frederick spied a house through the trees. Frederick thought it must be Wye House, the main house of the Lloyd plantation. Slaves called it the Great House Farm.

When they reached the house, Frederick's grandmother told him to play with the other children. This was the first time Frederick met his brother, Perry, and his sisters Eliza and Sarah.

A little while later, Frederick looked around. He didn't see Grandmother anywhere. He checked in the kitchen. He peered down the long driveway. How could she have gone off and left him? Frederick threw himself down onto the dusty ground and wailed. Perry handed Frederick a peach to comfort him. Frederick threw the peach as hard and as far as he could.

That night, Frederick cried himself to sleep. Slaveowners didn't give slaves beds in which to sleep, so he lay shivering on a hard, clay floor. During the early years of his life, Frederick had barely understood what it meant to be a slave. He had enough food to eat, places to play, and grandparents who cared for him. Frederick knew those days were over.

The next morning, Frederick ate cornmeal mush out of a hog trough with the other children. He had no spoon, so Frederick used his hands. He noticed other children using a shell to scoop up the mush. But there was not enough mush to fill them up.

Because Frederick was too young to work in the fields, he was given only a long shirt to wear. The overseer gave Frederick chores to do around the house. During the day, Frederick chased crows out of the garden. In the evening, he fetched the cows from the pasture.

Frederick spent many hours with twelve-year-old Daniel Lloyd, Edward's youngest son. When Daniel went hunting, Frederick helped him find the birds he shot. Daniel taught Frederick how to hunt. But he also taught Frederick other lessons, probably without even knowing it. Frederick listened closely when Daniel spoke. Frederick had imitated the sounds of Grandmother Bailey's chickens. He now mimicked the speech of this wealthy white child.

Frederick's mother sometimes managed to visit him at night. This wasn't easy. After a long day of working in the fields, slaves came home to do their own washing, cooking, mending, and other household chores. Frederick loved his mother's visits. He cuddled into her tall, slender body as she lay next to him. She would talk or sing to him until he fell asleep. But when he awoke in the morning, she was gone. Frederick wished she could stay longer. Each morning, Harriet was summoned to the fields by the overseer's horn. If she failed to be there, she was beaten with a hickory stick or a thick piece of cowhide.

Beatings were common on the plantation. Frederick once saw Aaron Anthony, his master, whip his Aunt Hester because she had disobeyed. Anthony whipped her until her entire back dripped with blood. Frederick hid in a closet, thinking he would be next.

When Frederick was about seven years old, his mother died. He hadn't even known that she was ill. The overseers did not allow Frederick to see her before she died.

Without his mother's visits to look forward to, one day blended into the next for Frederick. Months later, Frederick was told to run errands for Aaron Anthony's daughter, Lucretia. Lucretia realized that Frederick was bright and took him under her wing. She often brought food to Frederick. Lucretia and her husband, Thomas Auld, resolved to give Frederick a better life.

With her father's permission, they sent eight-year-old Frederick to live in Baltimore with Thomas's brother, Hugh, and his wife, Sophia. Lucretia gave Frederick his first pair of pants for his trip to Baltimore. She told him that he had to be clean to wear the pants. So Frederick spent his last day on the plantation in the Tuckahoe Creek. Wanting to please Lucretia, he scrubbed his feet and knees until they were sore.

While he scrubbed, Frederick thought about going to Baltimore. He had no idea what to expect. But he had seen what the future held for him on the Lloyd plantation. He hoped that things would be better in Baltimore.

2

Determined to Read

Frederick sailed for Baltimore on a Saturday morning. He took one last look at Edward Lloyd's plantation. Frederick would miss his few friends there. Nevertheless, he hoped it would be the last time he saw the plantation.

On Sunday morning, the boat docked at Smith's Wharf in Baltimore. A deckhand walked Frederick to the Aulds' home. When Frederick arrived, both Hugh and Sophia greeted him with joy. Perhaps here he could be part of a family again. He very much wanted Sophia to like him.

Even though Frederick was only eight years old, the Aulds gave him the job of caring for Tommy, their two-year-old son. Sophia told Tommy that this was "his Freddy." Frederick kept close watch on the toddler and made sure he did not wander into busy Philpot Street.

Sophia had never kept a slave in her home before. She treated Frederick like her own child. Each day, she read from her Bible, with Tommy on her lap and Frederick standing beside her. Frederick listened to Sophia read and watched her lips as she formed each word. Frederick asked Sophia to teach him to read. She started with the ABCs. Before long Frederick could read simple words.

Frederick loved living with Hugh and Sophia. But when Frederick was about nine, something happened to remind him that he was still a slave. His owner, Aaron Anthony, died. Therefore, all of Anthony's property—including the slaves—had to be divided among his children. Frederick didn't want to go back to Edward Lloyd's plantation, but he had no choice. For the first time in his life, Frederick started thinking about freedom. If he were free this wouldn't be happening to him.

Frederick cried when he said good-bye to Hugh and Sophia. They cried along with him. Frederick was terrified. What would happen to him? Lucretia had died while Frederick was in Baltimore. Luckily,

Lucretia's husband, Thomas, inherited Frederick. He decided to send him back to Baltimore. Frederick was overjoyed to be moving back to Hugh and Sophia. Sophia warmly welcomed back their Freddy.

Soon after, Hugh found out that Frederick had learned to read. He was furious. Frederick overheard him scolding Sophia. "If you teach a slave how to read, there will be no keeping him," Hugh said.

Frederick took Hugh's words to heart. So that was the key to freedom, he thought. He became more determined than ever to improve his reading. And if Sophia would not teach him, he would find others who would.

By the time Frederick was thirteen, he was old enough to work in the shipyards. Because he was a slave, Frederick was required to hand all of his wages over to Hugh Auld. But the job offered other opportunities. At the shipyards Frederick befriended a group of white boys. Frederick knew the boys could read and made a deal with them. The boys were always hungry, so Frederick gave them bread from his master's house. In return, they gave him reading lessons.

On Sundays, Frederick would wander down to the waterfront to meet his friends. They spent the day talking or fighting. Sometimes they read to each other.

One day Frederick and the others listened as one of the boys read from a book called *Columbian Orator.* It was a collection of speeches and poems. Some of them spoke of the evils of slavery. Listening made Frederick eager for more.

Frederick wanted his own copy of the *Orator.* He asked Hugh if he could keep some of the money he earned. Hugh agreed, as long as Frederick paid for his clothing and necessary tools. When Frederick had saved fifty cents, he bought the *Columbian Orator.* Frederick walked to the wharf and hid behind the ships. He read for hours.

One day on the wharf, Frederick helped two men unload a shipment of stone. One of the men asked Frederick if he was a slave for life. When Frederick answered yes, the men told him he should run away to the North, where there was no slavery. Frederick did not trust the men, so he acted uninterested.

Later, Frederick couldn't stop thinking about their conversation. Frederick had read stories about slaves who had escaped. But he had also read the stories of slaves who were caught and returned to their masters for a reward. Frederick knew that running away was dangerous. He might starve to death or drown. He could even be killed. But it would be worth the risk. He started to think about how he might escape.

When Frederick was fifteen, his life took another turn. Hugh Auld and his brother Thomas argued. They were unable to resolve their differences, and Thomas claimed his rightful ownership of Frederick. He took Frederick from Baltimore to the town of St. Michaels, Maryland. Thomas lived there with his new wife.

This time Frederick did not mind leaving Hugh and Sophia. Hugh had become hardened by drinking. Sophia had become more of a slave master. And he would be going to live with Thomas Auld, who had helped Frederick in the past. Still, Frederick would miss the white children who had taught him how to read. Frederick also regretted not running away while he was in Baltimore. Less than fifty miles north sat the free state of Pennsylvania. His new home was farther south, across the Chesapeake Bay.

But as Frederick and Thomas sailed down the bay to St. Michaels, Frederick paid close attention to the route the steamboats took to Philadelphia. The boats traveled northeast, up the bay. Frederick knew which way to run.

3

A Step Back

Thomas seemed to like and respect Frederick. But Frederick wasn't sure how he felt about Thomas. He believed that Thomas was a good person, but how could a good person justify owning slaves?

Soon after arriving in St. Michaels, Frederick began going to Methodist prayer meetings with some of the other slaves. The religion preached that all people are equal in the eyes of God. This gave Frederick hope. Anyone who really believed this could not support slavery.

When Thomas converted to the religion, Frederick was thrilled. Maybe Thomas would free his slaves, Frederick thought. But that was not the case. A few months later, Thomas and a group of white men broke up a bible study meeting that Frederick had organized. White people generally did not allow slaves to hold meetings. They were afraid that the group would plan to rebel or escape. From then on, Thomas labeled Frederick a troublemaker.

After Frederick had worked for Thomas for nine months, Thomas sent him to work for Edward Covey. It was common for slaveholders to rent slaves to other farmers. But Thomas chose Edward because of his well-known ability to make slaves obey—by beating them severely and making them work long hours in the hot sun.

Frederick had been with Edward about one week when his master told him to gather wood using a team of unbroken oxen. Frederick had no experience with oxen, much less untamed oxen. The animals turned over the cart and nearly crushed Frederick. Frederick went to the house and told Edward what had happened. He thought his master might feel sorry for him. Instead, Edward marched Frederick back to the woods. Edward tore off Frederick's clothes and whipped him until his back ran with blood. This was just the first of many beatings.

For the first time in his life, Frederick worked in the fields. He had never known such exhausting physical labor. He and the other slaves plowed and tended the corn and wheat fields from before sunup until sundown. They worked every day except Sundays, in all types of weather. At harvesttime, they often worked until midnight. There was enough food to eat. But there was rarely enough time to eat it.

After about six months of regular beatings and exhausting labor, Frederick began to feel himself crumble under his master's cruelty. Frederick's whole body ached from long days in the fields. And the regular beatings not only hurt physically, they also wore down his pride. Frederick no longer cared about reading. He lost his will to escape. He almost lost his will to live.

But no matter how low Frederick's spirits sank, the sight of white sailboats drifting across Chesapeake Bay always filled him with hope. He dreamed of standing on the deck of one of those boats. He even imagined himself swimming across the water. Frederick decided that even if he died trying to escape, it would be better than living as a slave.

The next time Edward made a move to whip him, Frederick fought back. Edward asked Frederick if he "meant to persist in his resistance." Frederick told Edward, "You have used me like a brute for six months. And I am determined to be used so no longer."

Frederick threw Edward to the ground. The two men fought for nearly two hours. Edward never again laid a hand on Frederick.

Between Christmas and New Year's, the slaves did not have to work in the fields. Some made brooms or baskets. Others hunted rabbits and raccoons. Frederick spent his time plotting an escape.

In January of 1835, Thomas sent Frederick to work for another nearby farmer, William Freeland. Unlike Edward, William did not force his slaves to work beyond sundown. And he gave them enough time to eat their meals.

Before long, the other slaves discovered that Frederick knew how to read. Though they could be whipped for learning, two of Frederick's friends begged him to teach them. The eager students found some old spelling books. Frederick brought out the *Columbian Orator.* Every Sunday and three nights a week for almost a year, Frederick taught other slaves to read under an old oak tree. Sometimes as many as forty people showed up. Frederick was thrilled. Reading, he knew, could unlock the door to freedom. The word he wanted them all to grasp was one he had learned at the docks in Baltimore—*abolition.*

Although Frederick's life had improved since he went to work for William, he still resolved to escape.

He wanted to take some of his friends with him. They all knew the danger, but freedom was worth the risk.

The five men planned to leave the Saturday night before Easter. They would steal a large canoe from a nearby plantation and then paddle seventy miles up the Chesapeake Bay toward Baltimore. It was safer to go by boat, Frederick thought. Anyone who saw them might think they were fishing. Near Baltimore, they would abandon the canoe and walk into Pennsylvania. Pennsylvania was a free state, but Frederick did not feel that they would be safe unless they walked to Canada.

Frederick lay awake worrying most of Friday night. The next morning, the men headed for the fields as usual. As Frederick worked, he suddenly had a feeling that he was going to be caught trying to escape. He whispered to his friend Sandy, "We are betrayed."

Soon the horn blew for breakfast. The men trudged to the house. Frederick was too nervous to eat. As he sat at the table, he saw four white men on horseback approach the house. The men walked in and grabbed Frederick and two of his friends. The men tied the captives' hands together and dragged them behind horses fifteen miles to the jail. The men had some-how learned of the escape plan and determined that Frederick was the ringleader.

Frederick was certain he would be hanged. The rebellion of a slave named Nat Turner in nearby Virginia in 1831 was still fresh in people's minds. Turner had led nearly seventy slaves to rebel. They killed sixty whites, including Turner's owner and his family. Turner and about twenty of the slaves had been hanged. Angry whites killed one hundred innocent slaves in response. As a result, slaves caught trying to escape were hanged as a warning to those thinking about leaving.

So Frederick could not believe his eyes when Thomas Auld arrived at the jail to fetch him. Thomas seemed to care about Frederick. He knew that the tall, powerful seventeen-year-old was strong-willed. He feared that Frederick would be killed. So Thomas sent Frederick back to his brother, Hugh, in Baltimore. Thomas told Frederick that if he worked at a trade until he was twenty-five, he could have his freedom. But Frederick wasn't sure he could wait that long.

Back in Baltimore, Hugh sent Frederick to work in a shipyard once again. Within two years, Frederick learned to caulk, or fix holes in ships. Soon he was earning a dollar and a half a day—a decent wage for the time. As he had before, Frederick handed over his wages to his master.

27

At the shipyard, Frederick became friends with the free black men with whom he worked. His coworkers introduced Frederick to the East Baltimore Mental Improvement Society. The society was one of many groups dedicated to promoting respect and intellect among black people in the city. Frederick learned how to debate ideas. At one of the society's meetings, Frederick met Anna Murray, a free black woman who worked as a housekeeper. The two grew very close.

Attending the society meetings helped build Frederick's confidence. He continued to plan his escape. He only regretted having to say good-bye to his friends, especially Anna. Frederick refused to allow his fears of getting caught to interrupt his planning. He began trying to save some of the money Hugh allowed him to keep for his escape.

Frederick worked night and day from May until August. Little by little, he was able to save enough to buy train tickets. Frederick chose the date on which he would escape—Monday, September 3, 1838.

Frederick had three weeks before he left. He did not want Hugh to suspect his plans. So the next week, Frederick again turned over all of his wages to Hugh. Hugh was so pleased he handed Frederick twenty-five cents. He said, "Now make good use of that, Frederick." Fredrick knew that he would.

One important part of Frederick's escape plan was the Underground Railroad. The so-called railroad was a secret network of people who helped slaves escape to freedom. People along the railroad's route hid slaves in their homes and helped transport them from one site to the next. Frederick had helped many others escape via the railroad. Now he would use the network himself.

On September 3, as he had planned, Frederick got up early. He had borrowed a sailor's uniform and seaman's papers from one of the free black sailors he'd met at the wharf. Wearing a red shirt, a kerchief around his neck, and a flat broad-brimmed hat, Frederick rode to the train station in a friend's carriage. To avoid having his papers checked, Frederick waited until the train was just about to leave. Then he ran and jumped aboard. His heart raced as he found a seat in the black section. The train was going fast, but for Frederick it was not fast enough. He had boarded the train safely, but at any moment he could be discovered and turned over to slave catchers.

Despite a couple of close calls, Frederick made it to Wilmington, Delaware, without harm. There he caught a steamboat to Philadelphia. To be a safe distance from his possible captors, he continued by ferry to New York City.

On the morning of September 4, sleepy and in a daze, Frederick took a walk down Broadway Avenue. He had made it to a free state, but legally he was still a slave. Slave hunters might try to capture him.

Hungry and lonely, Frederick wandered the streets. He was supposed to go to the home of David Ruggles, a man who had helped many runaways. But he had no idea how to find the address written on the slip of paper in his pocket. He was afraid to ask directions. That night, feeling more alone than ever, Frederick slept behind some barrels on a wharf.

When Frederick woke up, he started walking again. After several blocks, he found himself standing in front of the jail. He looked across the street and saw a sailor. Still in his sailor's uniform, Frederick found the courage to ask the man for help. The sailor took Frederick in for the night. The next morning, he walked Frederick to David Ruggles's door.

Once Frederick was safely settled, he wrote to Anna. He told her he had arrived in New York and he begged her to join him. Then Frederick changed his last name from Bailey to Johnson to fool anyone who might be chasing him. Soon Anna arrived in New York. David Ruggles contacted the Reverend James Pennington, who was also a runaway slave. The reverend married Frederick and Anna on September 15,

1838. Anna, wearing a plum-colored silk dress, looked up at her handsome, young husband. Frederick smiled with pride at his new wife.

With the money David gave them for a wedding gift, the couple bought two train tickets to New Bedford, Massachusetts. New Bedford was the perfect city for a young black couple. As the center of the booming whaling industry, the city offered plenty of jobs. Black and white children attended school together. Many churches welcomed black worshipers.

On his third day in New Bedford, Frederick found a job. He had tried to get work as a caulker. But some white workers refused to work alongside a black man. He realized then that prejudice was as prevalent in the North as it was in the South. But Frederick needed work, so he cut wood for a dollar per day. Eventually, Frederick found a more permanent job filling ships with oil. It was hard work, but Frederick loved knowing that he was earning money for himself and Anna.

Soon Frederick and Anna found that New Bedford was not all that it seemed. At mixed churches, for example, black worshipers had to sit in a separate section. Frederick would not tolerate such humiliation. Instead he joined the all-black Zion Methodist Church, where he started preaching. Frederick realized that when he stood up and spoke, everyone listened. With his strong voice, dark eyes, and six-foot-two-inch stature, Frederick commanded attention.

Through the church, Anna and Frederick met many new friends. Two of the couple's first friends in New Bedford were Mary and Nathan Johnson. Nathan suggested that Frederick choose a different last name. There were too many Johnsons in New Bedford. Nathan remembered the name "Douglas" from a Sir Walter Scott poem. Frederick liked the name. He added another *s*, and Frederick Johnson became Frederick Douglass.

Frederick had not been in New Bedford long when a man knocked on his door. He was selling subscriptions to William Lloyd Garrison's antislavery newspaper, the *Liberator.* Garrison, a white man, saw slavery as evil, and he devoted his life to abolishing it. Frederick barely earned enough to feed himself and Anna, who was pregnant with their first child. But the man offered Frederick a free trial subscription.

Inspired by the *Liberator,* Frederick felt more and more compelled to speak out against slavery. On March 12, 1839, Frederick stood up at a church meeting and spoke. He said that slaves should not be sent back to Africa, as some believed. And he said that all slaves should be freed. The *Liberator* reported that Frederick "spoke eloquently."

4

A Powerful Speaker

Frederick and Anna's first child was born on June 24, 1839. They named her Rosetta. And on October 9, 1840, Anna gave birth to a son, named Lewis Henry.

The next year, Frederick and Anna moved their growing family to a larger house at 111 Ray Street. That summer Anna spent much of her time hoeing in the garden, caring for the two children, and preparing for the arrival of a third child. In the evenings, Frederick entertained his family by playing the music of Handel, Haydn, and Mozart on his violin.

During this time, Frederick began to gain experience as an abolitionist speaker. On August 16, 1841, Frederick spoke at the Massachusetts Anti-Slavery Convention in Nantucket. The Big Shop, where the meeting was held, was so full that people stood outside and peered in the windows. Some even sat on the rafters. After a somewhat hesitant beginning, Frederick spoke for two hours. The audience barely breathed while Frederick spoke of his life as a slave.

When the meeting was over, John Collins asked Frederick to tour as a speaker for the Massachusetts Anti-Slavery Society. He would share the platform with Stephen S. Foster, another abolitionist. Frederick only had to repeat the story he had just told. For Frederick this was a dream come true. After years of following orders, he would finally be doing something he wanted to do. And he would be paid for it.

In the fall of 1841, the Douglass family moved to Lynn, Massachusetts, a small town north of Boston. Frederick felt safer there than in the big city. And he was only a short train ride away from the Anti-Slavery Society's headquarters in Boston. The group helped him buy his house in Lynn.

Just after the move, Frederick joined another speaking tour. This time he traveled with William Lloyd Garrison, publisher of the *Liberator,* and other abolitionists, including Parker Pillsbury, Stephen Foster, and Abby Kelly. Frederick was quickly gaining a reputation as an eloquent speaker with a sharp mind.

Frederick looked for ways to do more. In 1843 he volunteered for a tour of one hundred conventions. Sponsored by the American Anti-Slavery Society, the project aimed to present one hundred antislavery meetings across the country. Frederick nearly reached the goal single-handedly as he traveled through New England, upstate New York, Ohio, Indiana, and Pennsylvania. He spoke at meeting halls and churches. He slept in shabby rooms. More than once, his speech was disrupted by an angry mob. In Indiana, a crowd beat him badly. He was lucky to escape with just a broken hand.

For a time, it seemed as if Frederick's ability as a speaker worked against him. Because he spoke so eloquently, some people doubted that he had in fact been a slave. If he had lived as a slave, they asked, how had he learned to speak so well? To prove that the stories he told were true, Frederick wrote a book about his life as a slave. In June 1845, at the age of twenty-seven, Frederick published his autobiography. Five thousand copies of *Narrative Life of Frederick Douglass* were printed. They sold out almost immediately. French and German editions were printed, as well as nine editions in England.

In the book, Frederick named his former owner, putting himself in great danger. His master would know where Frederick lived and could easily send a slave catcher to bring him back. Frederick decided it would be wise to move away from Lynn. Frederick left his family in the United States and sailed to the British Isles.

Frederick was a popular speaker throughout Great Britain. People traveled for miles to hear him. Sometimes after a speech, as many as one thousand people stood in line just to shake his hand. But some people criticized Frederick for not sticking to anti-slavery issues. In speeches and in a letter to the *Liberator,* he exposed the horrible working conditions of the poor in England, Ireland, and Scotland. He replied, "I am not only an American slave, but a man, and as such, am bound to use my powers for the welfare of the whole human brotherhood."

In 1846 William Lloyd Garrison joined Frederick in Great Britain for a speaking tour. The trip was a great success. When William returned home, Frederick was sad to see him go. William's departure made him miss home even more.

By the fall of 1846, Frederick was ready to return home himself. However, there was the possibility that Hugh Auld would reclaim him as a slave. So a group of British abolitionists contacted Hugh and asked him to sell Frederick to them. Hugh agreed. They collected the $710.96 necessary to free him. On December 5, 1846, Hugh signed Frederick's release papers. When twenty-eight-year-old Frederick stepped off the ship and onto American soil, he was a free man once and for all.

5

Freedom for All

Frederick returned from England with renewed determination to fight against slavery and to stand up for the rights of black people. While in Britain, Frederick had mentioned to friends the idea of starting his own newspaper. They had encouraged him with enthusiasm. But when Frederick told his abolitionist friends in the United States, they strongly discouraged him. William Lloyd Garrison reasoned that there were too many abolitionist papers already available. Frederick's paper would never survive the competition. William was also worried about how Frederick's paper would affect the *Liberator.*

Frederick dismissed the idea for the moment. In August 1847, Frederick and William began a speaking tour of the United States. After the warm welcome they had received in Britain, Frederick was shocked by how they were treated. At times, audiences were hateful and violent. When Frederick returned home, he decided to start his own newspaper after all. The hostility he had faced while on the tour convinced him that the paper was necessary. Frederick's decision greatly damaged his friendship with William. William felt betrayed. The two men were never again as close as they had been.

Frederick called his newspaper *North Star.* Slaves escaping to freedom used the North Star to guide them. He turned out the first issue on December 3, 1847. The words on the masthead read, "Right is of no Sex—Truth is of no Color." The paper featured articles, poems, and essays by black writers. Articles also highlighted the achievements of black people. For the first time in his life, Frederick felt free to make his own decisions and to voice his opinions. And he had opinions—not only about slavery, but about women's rights, working conditions, and other issues.

After the newspaper was up and running, Frederick decided to move his family to Rochester, New York. If he stayed in Massachusetts, the *North Star* would have to compete with the *Liberator* for sales. And Frederick didn't want to add to William's anger. Rochester was known as an antislavery town. The Female Anti-Slavery Society and other abolitionists were located there. Once again, Anna packed up the children and all their belongings.

In Rochester, Frederick met regularly with the Female Anti-Slavery Society. Members of this group included women's rights advocates Elizabeth Cady Stanton and Susan B. Anthony. Frederick found that the rights for which he was fighting were similar to those for which women were fighting. In most places, women could not own property. Wages earned by a woman belonged to her husband (or father if she was not married). They could not attend college or hold certain jobs.

Frederick also focused on the paper. He had plenty of support from women's rights advocates. The *North Star* garnered a number of glowing reviews. Unfortunately, praise did not translate into money. It wasn't long before the two-dollar annual subscription rate did not cover the cost of expenses. In the spring of 1848, the need for money forced Frederick to return to the lecture circuit. He was on the road for six months. But he refused to give up publishing the paper.

Despite his financial difficulties, Frederick remained devoted to the causes in which he believed. He attended the women's rights convention in Seneca Falls, New York. Held on July 20, 1848, the convention was the first such gathering in the world. Elizabeth Cady Stanton led the discussion on the issue of women's right to vote. Many women thought that asking for the right to vote was asking for too much, too soon. It looked as if the resolution was heading for defeat. Elizabeth asked Frederick to speak. Everyone in the audience leaned forward to hear his words. Frederick compared his struggles as a slave to the difficulties faced by women. The two groups shared many of the same issues. When the final vote was taken, the resolution passed.

On March 22, 1849, Frederick and Anna's fifth child, Annie, was born. This new addition to the family made Frederick look for a house in the country. He bought a place with a large yard just outside of Rochester. There was plenty of room for the children to play. Anna planted a garden, and Frederick even planted fruit trees. The house was spacious, too. Before long, the house became a major stop on the Underground Railroad. A hidden crawl space on the second floor allowed the family to hide as many as eleven slaves at one time.

During this time, Frederick was most proud of his work on the *North Star.* The newspaper still did not bring in much money, but publishing the paper made Frederick feel independent and powerful. And the *North Star* was the most important outlet for black writers and abolitionists of the time.

By June of 1851, the *North Star* had sunk deeper into debt. Frederick agreed to merge the *North Star* with the *Liberty Party Paper,* a publication supported by Garrit Smith. Frederick continued to control the paper's content. Smith paid the cost of running the paper. The co-owners changed the paper's name to *Frederick Douglass' Paper.*

In 1852 the Rochester Ladies' Anti-Slavery Society asked Frederick to speak at their Independence Day celebration. His words were not gentle. He said: "My subject, fellow citizens, is American slavery. This Fourth of July is yours, not mine. You may rejoice; I must mourn." He called the people of the United States barbarians for tolerating slavery. When he sat down, the audience stood and cheered.

Frederick had found two things he loved to do—speaking and writing. He continued to devote endless hours to both. In 1855 he published his second autobiography, *My Bondage and My Freedom.* In the book, Frederick updated readers on his life experiences after his escape to the North. He also discussed, with great intelligence, the injustices of slavery.

In his travels and work, Frederick often met with other abolition leaders. One of the most intense was John Brown. John was a white man who worked hard to end slavery. Frederick respected John for his courage and for his ideas. But the two men had very different approaches to the slavery problem. John felt that since slavery was a violent act, it should be met with violence. Frederick did not believe in using violence to achieve his goals. He liked to say, "Murder is no cure for murder."

For three weeks in February of 1858, John stayed with Frederick and Anna. Frederick listened as John talked of his plans to capture the United States Arsenal at Harpers Ferry, Virginia, and encourage slaves to rebel. John asked Frederick to join him, but in the end Frederick decided that he could not support the plan.

On October 17, 1859, John and eighteen followers raided the arsenal. The plan went astray when the local militia surrounded the arsenal. John and some of his followers were hanged for treason. Since Frederick had written to John, Frederick feared he might be arrested and brought to trial. He left his family behind and fled to Canada. From there, he sailed to Great Britain, where he launched another successful speaking tour.

While Frederick was in Great Britain, tensions were rising in the United States between antislavery groups and proslavery groups. Shortly after Abraham

Lincoln took office in 1861, six Southern states broke away from the other states and declared themselves an independent country. President Lincoln refused to allow the nation to be divided. The Civil War began on April 12, 1861, when Southern troops fired the first shot against the Union at Fort Sumter.

President Lincoln did not see the war as a way to end slavery, but Frederick did. Despite his objection to violence, Frederick welcomed the Civil War. He felt it would bring about freedom for slaves in the South and a better life for free blacks in the North. While battles raged in the South, Frederick insisted in his speeches and newspaper editorials that the aim of the war must be to abolish slavery.

On September 22, 1862, President Lincoln issued a statement called the Emancipation Proclamation. It said that if the Southern troops did not surrender by January 1, 1863, he would issue a proclamation that would free all slaves in the rebelling states. Three thousand people gathered in Tremont Temple in Boston on January 1, 1863, to wait for the South's response. Frederick was asked to speak. The crowd waited all day and into the night. Finally at around eleven o'clock, word came that the South would continue to fight. Lincoln's proclamation went into effect. The document stated, "I do order and declare that all persons held as slaves within said designated States and parts of States are, and henceforward shall be, free." Everyone in the Tremont Temple threw their hats into the air and shouted for joy. Frederick's voice was among the loudest.

The Emancipation Proclamation also stated that black men could fight as soldiers in the war. Frederick was quick to recruit young black men. He even enlisted two of his sons, Charles and Lewis.

During the war, some two hundred thousand black soldiers and sailors were called to battle. However, fewer than one hundred blacks became officers. In addition, the black soldiers often did not receive pay and benefits equal to that of the whites. This angered Frederick. In July 1863, he traveled to Washington, D.C., to share his complaints with President Lincoln. The president listened with respect. But he told Frederick that change would only come about slowly. Frederick then met with Secretary of War Edwin M. Stanton. Stanton offered to pay Frederick to recruit black soldiers. Frederick quickly agreed.

Frederick ceased publication of his newspaper, which had come to be called *Douglass' Monthly*. He wrote his last editorial on August 16, 1863. Then he waited to hear from Stanton about his commission. He wrote to Stanton, but he received no response.

Finally Frederick gave up. Still eager to fill the army's ranks with black recruits, Frederick continued recruiting on his own, without one cent of pay.

When Lincoln was elected for his second term, Frederick decided to attend the inauguration and reception at the White House. Two guards tried to keep Frederick out. But Lincoln spotted Frederick and said, "Here comes my friend Douglass!"

In 1865, five days after the Civil War ended with a Union victory, Lincoln was shot and killed. Frederick gathered with friends and neighbors to mourn. He talked of his love and admiration for the fallen president. Mary Todd Lincoln sent Frederick her husband's walking stick. Frederick collected them, and Mrs. Lincoln said her husband would have wanted him to have it.

On January 31, 1865, Congress passed the Thirteenth Amendment, which officially abolished slavery. In 1866 Frederick and the Convention of Colored Men met with President Andrew Johnson to ask that blacks be granted the right to vote. Without the vote, Frederick argued, freedom was an empty victory. But the group was unable to convince the president. It was not until March 30, 1870, that a different president, Ulysses S. Grant, signed the Fifteenth Amendment, giving blacks the right to vote.

To Live Respectably

By this time, Frederick had become a wealthy man—mostly from lecturing and sales of his books. (It helped, too, that Anna was good at managing money.) But Frederick wanted more than wealth. He had dedicated his whole life to working for the abolition of slavery. He had spent months away from his home and family while on speaking tours. And he had worked hard to promote literacy among blacks. Frederick had accomplished a great deal. But even after slavery was abolished, Frederick continued to devote time to the causes in which he believed. He began to fight for equal rights for women.

He supported an amendment to the Constitution that would grant women the right to vote. In 1870, Frederick purchased another newspaper, the *New National Era*. The paper promoted the rights of women and blacks.

During this time, Frederick began to consider running for public office. He spent more time in Washington, D.C. Rosetta and her husband, Nathan, moved into the country house to be with Anna. One night in June 1872, Rosetta awoke to the smell of smoke. Neighbors, seeing the flames, rushed to help carry books, pictures, and furniture (even the piano) out of the house. The house burned to the ground.

Frederick returned from Washington the next day. He was thankful to find his family safe, but he was saddened to see that even the fruit trees had burned. Rather than face the task of rebuilding, Frederick moved his family to Washington. He had already located his newspaper there, and he took an active role in the city. He campaigned hard for President Grant's reelection in 1872. When Grant won, Frederick thought Grant might appoint him to a government position. But that did not happen.

Instead, in March 1874, Frederick became president of the Freedman's Savings and Trust Company.

Before Frederick took over, however, the bank had made bad investments and loaned money to people who could not pay it back. Frederick tried to turn things around, but he was eventually forced to close the bank. Many people—mostly blacks—who had trusted Frederick lost their hard-earned money. Frederick felt awful. Around this time, Frederick was also forced to shut down his newspaper. He had always struggled with finding enough subscribers, and he decided to focus his energy elsewhere.

As he approached age sixty, Frederick again sought political appointments. This time he received them. In 1877 President Rutherford B. Hayes appointed Frederick marshal of the District of Columbia. He was the first black man to serve in this post. One of the customary jobs of the marshal was to stand next to the president at formal receptions and introduce each guest. But President Hayes did not ask Frederick to do this. Frederick felt slighted, but what could he do? The president did put Frederick in charge of government jobs. Frederick saw to it that many of those well-paying jobs went to blacks.

As a birthday gift for Anna, Frederick bought a new house in the hills above Washington, D.C. Anna had been ill with pneumonia. When she felt strong enough, she would sit in her wheelchair and enjoy the view. The house overlooked the Anacostia River, and she could see the capitol in the distance. Anna loved the house and the flower and vegetable gardens that surrounded it. Frederick loved the house, too. Every day he walked the six miles to the capitol and back to his home. Seeing his house at the end of the day filled Frederick with a sense of pride.

In 1881 President James A. Garfield appointed Frederick recorder of deeds for the District of Columbia. He was responsible for the city's land ownership records. Away from work, Frederick continued to write and speak. That same year, Frederick published his third autobiography, *Life and Times of Frederick Douglass.* He wrote it so that people would not forget about slavery and the damage it had done.

In the summer of 1882, Anna suffered a stroke. The stroke paralyzed the left side of her body. She struggled to learn to speak again. Frederick brought in the best nurses to care for her, but she never regained her health. On the morning of August 4, Anna died at the age of sixty-nine.

Following Anna's death, Frederick was sad and lonely. He almost suffered a nervous breakdown. But he pulled himself together by continuing to speak on behalf of black Americans and women. He was in constant demand.

On January 24, 1884, Frederick married Helen Pitts. He had hired her as a clerk when he worked in the recorder of deeds office. Helen Pitts was nearly twenty years younger than Frederick, and she was white. She was active in the women's rights movement and had published her own feminist newspaper.

The marriage caused a tremendous stir across the country. Frederick told people that their marriage proved that whites and blacks could live together as equals. Not everyone disapproved, however. Elizabeth Cady Stanton sent her best wishes. She wrote: "If a good man from Maryland sees fit to marry a disfranchised woman from New York, there should be no legal impediments to the union." (disfranchised means denied the right to vote). Frederick seemed to enjoy the controversy his marriage stirred. He was fond of saying: "My first wife was the color of my mother, and the second, the color of my father."

Frederick and Helen shared a love of music. In the evenings, Helen would often play the piano while Frederick accompanied her on the violin. The couple went together to women's rights meetings and to literary gatherings, where Frederick performed dramatic readings. In September 1886, the couple visited Egypt, Italy, Greece, and Africa. At the end of the trip, Frederick spoke at a few events in London.

When he returned to the United States, Frederick turned his attention to the problem of the extreme poverty of blacks in the South. In the spring of 1888, he traveled to Georgia and South Carolina. He was appalled by what he saw. Black sharecroppers lived in terrible conditions. Frederick blamed the government. He started to campaign for candidates who ran against those already in power.

In 1889 President Benjamin Harrison appointed Frederick as minister and consul to Haiti. Frederick's friends believed that this was the government's way of getting Frederick out of the country. Others thought that he could accomplish much more at home, fighting for freedom and equal rights. Frederick, however, believed it was an honor he could not turn down.

In Haiti, Frederick found that the people admired and respected him. But he was in a difficult spot. Frederick's appointment came during a time of great growth in the Caribbean. Frederick tried to serve what he thought to be the United States' best interests. He refused to exploit the Haitian people, however. This put him at odds with the aims of the United States government. In the end, neither the press nor the American people looked on Frederick's Haitian appointment favorably. In 1891 Frederick resigned from the office and returned to America. On February 20, 1895, Frederick died at home of a heart attack. He had spent the day at a meeting of the National Council of Women. Hundreds of people visited the Metropolitan African Methodist Episcopal Church in Washington, D.C., where his body lay in state. He was buried at the family plot in Mount Hope Cemetery in Rochester, New York.

In Washington, black public schools closed for the day. Around the world, newspapers praised Frederick's accomplishments. Some newspapers ran the headline: "Friend and champion of women dies." The *London Daily News* wrote, "From first to last his was a noble life. His own people have lost a father and a friend, and all good men have lost a comrade in the fight for the legal emancipation of one race and the spiritual emancipation of all."

Bibliography

Blassingame, John W. *Frederick Douglass: The Clarion Voice.* Washington, DC: National Park Service, 1976.

Davis, William C., ed. *Civil War Journal: The Leaders.* Nashville: Rutledge Hill, 1997.

Douglass, Frederick. *Life and Times of Frederick Douglass.* 1892. Reprint, New York: Gramercy Books, 1993.

Douglass, Frederick. *My Bondage and My Freedom.* 1855. Adapted by Barbara Ritchie. New York: Crowell Publishing, 1966.

Douglass, Frederick. *Narrative of the Life of Frederick Douglass, an American Slave.* 1845. Reprint, New York: Laurel Books, 1997.

Huggins, Nathan Irvin. *Slave and Citizen; the Life of Frederick Douglass.* Boston: Little Brown and Company, 1980.

McFeely, William S. *Frederick Douglass.* New York: W.W. Norton & Company, 1991.

Meltzer, Milton, ed. *Frederick Douglass, In His Own Words.* San Diego: Harcourt Brace, 1995.

Websites

American Visionaries: Frederick Douglass
<http://www.cr.nps.gov/csd/exhibits/douglass/>

Frederick Douglass National Historic Site
<http://www.nps.gov/frdo/freddoug.html>

Frederick Douglass Texts Online
<http://dir.yahoo.com/Arts/Humanities/History/
U_S__History/By_Time_Period/19th_C.../Texts>

Index of Frederick Douglass Historic Documents
<http://www.usc.edu/isd/archives/ethnicstudies/
historicdocs/Douglass/>

Index

abolition, 24, 33, 35–36, 38, 39, 40, 42, 44–45, 46, 49
American Anti-Slavery Society, 36–37
Anthony, Aaron, 8, 12, 13, 15
Anthony, Susan B., 41
Auld, Hugh, 13, 14–16, 18, 19, 26, 28, 38
Auld, Lucretia Anthony, 13, 15–16
Auld, Sophia, 13, 14–16, 19
Auld, Thomas, 13, 16, 19, 20–21, 24, 26

Bailey, Betsey (grandmother), 7–9, 11
Bailey, Frederick, 7–31. *See also* Johnson, Frederick; Douglass, Frederick
Bailey, Harriet (mother), 7–8, 12–13
Bailey, Isaac (grandfather), 9
Bailey, Perry (brother), 9, 11
Baltimore, Maryland, 13, 14–19, 24, 25, 26
black people's rights and suffrage, 39, 49, 50–51, 54.
Brown, John, 44–45

Collins, John, 36
Columbian Orator, 18, 24
Convention of Colored Men, 49
Covey, Edward, 21–22, 24

Douglass, Anna (wife), 33, 35–37, 42, 45, 50, 51, 53–54
Douglass, Annie (daughter), 42
Douglass, Charles (son), 47
Douglass, Frederick, 33–59: birth, 7–8; childhood, 7–11; education of, 15, 16, 18, 22, 24; escape from slavery, 18–31; in Europe, 56–57; and money, 18, 26, 28, 50; as editor, 39–41, 42–43, 47; political appointments of, 51, 53, 57–58; as public speaker, 32–33, 35–37, 41, 42, 44, 45, 46, 49, 54, 57; and recruitment of black soldiers, 47–48 religion and church of 20–21, 32, 33, 58; as slave, 12–28; and the Underground Railroad, 29, 42; and views on violence, 45, 46; and the women's movement, 41–42, 44, 58; in the workforce, 9, 11, 15, 16, 18, 21–22, 26, 32, 36, 51, 53, 54; as writer, 44, 53
Douglass, Helen Pitts (second wife), 56–57
Douglass, Lewis Henry (son), 35, 47
Douglass' Monthly, 47. *See also Frederick Douglass' Paper and North Star.*
Douglass, Rosetta (daughter), 35, 51

Emancipation Proclamation, 46–47

Female Anti-Slavery Society, 40–41
Fifteenth Amendment, 51
Frederick Douglass' Paper, 44. *See also North Star and Douglass' Monthly.*

Garfield, President James A., 54
Garrison, William Lloyd, 33, 36, 38, 39–40
Grant, President Ulysses S., 49, 51

Harrison, President Benjamin, 57
Hayes, President Rutherford B., 53

Johnson, President Andrew, 49
Johnson, Frederick. *See* Douglass, Frederick

Kelly, Abby, 36

Liberator, 33, 36, 38, 39, 40
Liberty Party Paper, 42
Life and Times of Frederick Douglass, 54
Lincoln, President Abraham, 45–46, 47, 49
Lincoln, Mary Todd, 49
Lloyd, Colonel Edward, 8, 9, 12, 14, 15

Massachusetts Anti-Slavery Convention, 35
Massachusetts Anti-Slavery Society, 36
Murray, Anna, 28, 31–33. See also Douglass, Anna
My Bondage and My Freedom, 44

Narrative Life of Frederick Douglass, 37
New Bedford, Massachusetts, 32–33
New National Era, 51, 53
North Star, 40, 41, 42, 43. *See also Frederick Douglass' Paper and Douglass' Monthly*

Pillsbury, Parker, 36

Rochester Ladies' Anti-Slavery Society, 44

Smith, Garrit, 44
Stanton, Edwin M., 47
Stanton, Elizabeth Cady, 41–42, 56
Thirteenth Amendment, 49
Turner, Nat, 26

Underground Railroad, 29, 42

Women's rights and suffrage, 40–42, 51, 54, 56, 58.

About the Author

Maryann N. Weidt was a children's librarian for twenty years. She lives with her husband in Duluth, Minnesota. She is also the author of *Oh, the Places He Went: A Story about Dr. Seuss*; *Stateswoman to the World: A Story about Eleanor Roosevelt*; *Mr. Blue Jeans: A Story about Levi Strauss*; and *Revolutionary Poet: A Story about Phillis Wheatley*, all published by Carolrhoda Books.

About the Illustrator

Jeni Reeves studied art and sculpture in Italy. She has worked in photography, television, and graphic and illustrative design in the United States and England. She has also spent a number of years living and working abroad. She lives in Iowa with her husband, Stuart, and daughter, Tegan. Jeni also illustrated *Colors of Kenya*, by Fran Sammis; *Babe Didrikson Zaharias: All Around Athlete*, by Jane Sutcliffe; *Booker T. Washington*, by Thomas Amper; and *The Girl Who Struck out Babe Ruth*, by Jean L. S. Patrick, all published by Carolrhoda Books.